Photoshop
Master the Basics

Top 12 Easy Photoshop Tips and Tricks For Beginners

James Carren

For more books by this author, please visit
www.photographybooks.us

Table of Contents

Introduction

Photoshop is at once a very, very complex tool, and yet is surprisingly easy to use once you get the hang of it. The same adage applies to it as it does to computers: Algorithms make up the program, and it simply responds by doing what you tell it to. When people run into problems, that's because they know what they want to do, but they don't know how to tell the program what to do. Luckily, Adobe is very helpful, and they have 24 hour online support for any jams you might find yourself in.

Before we get started, it is important to note that Photoshop updates with new versions quite a lot, and they really do get smoother and more streamlined with every change. Typically, if you're going back only one or two versions, you should still be okay to use the instructions in this manual, but just be aware that there might be small differences you have to account for. That said, I will be using Photoshop CC, or Creative Cloud for all of the instructions I present here.

This manual is likely going to be split into sections, a continuation from one book to the next. The table of contents will apply to the thing as a whole, so if you get to the end of this and you're wondering where the rest of it is, not to worry! The rest will be in part two.

In this section I want to focus on the very basics, so that you as a beginning user can kind of dip your toes in the water, so to speak. I'll be starting with the process of how you prepare an image and set up a workspace to your liking, and moving into navigating your toolbar, basic channels, layers and paths, adjustment layers, blend modes and levels and curves. I will explain what they are, what they do, and how to apply them for usage both as a correction and as an artistic application. Subsequent books will cover more advanced topics, really moving into finer control and more freedom of artistic application as opposed to correction. In my opinion, that's what Photoshop was really meant for anyway. So let's get started! By the end, I think you'll be pleased by how much more you can do with your images and how natural and not "Photoshopped" they look.

Chapter 1
Options for Setting Up Your Workspace and Preparing Images for Editing

Before you can get started working, you need to set up your workspace to your liking. I think of it just like a desk, and you want to make sure that it's optimized to your purposes and to your personal workflow.

Essentials

The way you access workspace options is via a small drop down menu in the upper right hand corner, which by default reads, Essentials. This is the workspace I normally use.

I would suggest pulling up your own Photoshop workspace as you read through this book to get the most out of it. Being able to see it in front of you will help comprehension greatly.

The tool which you are currently using will be highlighted in the upper left hand corner. This is also where you will find any presets you may have for that tool. Directly beneath this is the toolbox, which runs the whole length of the left side of your screen. I will explain what each tool does in the next chapter. Then you have your foreground, background indicator, which is represented by black and white unless you have selected a color with the picker. Beneath that is your go to button for a quick mask, and your full screen editing mode, which can be exited with the escape key.

Along the very, very top, you have your menus, which of course, as with word or any other computer program will locate all of the drop down menus you will need if you don't know the shortcuts. Speaking of shortcuts, I use Photoshop so much that I actually have a shortcut map keyboard cover. If you don't plan on customizing your shortcuts too much, I would definitely suggest investing in one. It's extremely helpful for learning on, and also just as a daily reminder.

Just below your menus bar, back in the actual Photoshop dialog, you will see a toolbar that becomes customized based on whichever tool you have selected. I will also go over these in Chapter 2, but I would still suggest scrolling through all your tools and experimenting with it on your own time too. If you ever get confused or can't remember what all these buttons do, you can always hover your mouse over them and Photoshop will tell you. This is also true of all your tools.

Moving to your right side, there are two boxes, one represented by an arrow and squares, and one by what looks like a bunch of differently shaped blocks. These are your history bar and your properties bar. The history bar will likely become your best friend, because instead of having to hit undo ten times when you really make a mistake, you can just select the history bar and click on the step you'd like to go back to. Easy! Be careful though, because even with the history bar, you can only go back so much before it makes you click to go back to your very original image. Properties, of course, will reflect whatever specs are relevant to your image.

Next to that, you've got your color and swatches dialog, which are pretty self explanatory. When you get into using the eyedropper tool, you'll find that you can use it directly within this dialog to select the colors you need.

Below are your Libraries, Adjustments, and Styles tabs, which, when selected, directly affect the menu below it. Libraries will allow you to connect to an online server and access your library directly, while Adjustments allows you to view all the adjustment layer symbols right there and thus makes it easier than using either the top or bottom drop down menus to apply them. Finally, Styles, which features all sorts of gradients you can choose from, create, and apply to your pictures. Finally, there are Layers, Channels, and Paths, which too have their own chapter, because this is the area of your workspace you will likely need to pay attention to the most, aside from which tool you have selected. The Essentials layout is the one that will be used for the remainder of tutorials after this chapter.

The Other Workspaces

Since we won't be using the other workspaces for these demos, I'll just give a little bit of information. 3D is useful if you are a graphic designer or 3D animator, and need to do some basic rendering. While other programs that are made specifically for these purposes do a much better job, the 3D workspace can be useful especially if you need to utilize Smart Objects, which will be addressed later. There are also spaces for Motion, Digital Painting, Photography, and Typography. Experiment with these as needed. The only real difference between Essentials and Photography workspaces is that the photography one features a histogram at the top of everything, kind of like in Lightroom. This can be useful when doing color and exposure corrections. You can also customize your workspace to include relevant elements of each of these standards.

Image Prep

Now that you have a small idea of how to navigate the workspace, let's talk about how to prepare an image for an editing job. When you first open an image for editing, you want it to be the highest quality type of file you can get. A CR2 or DNG file is preferable, because you'll get the most out of your image. If you didn't know, these file types are what is referred to as a RAW file. It contains more raw information straight from the camera sensor than any other file type, enabling you to pull more information from areas that might otherwise be unsalvageable If you didn't shoot in RAW this time, from now on you should. Just change the setting in your camera menu. If you are working with a RAW file, when you open the image, a dialog box for an extension called Camera Raw will automatically open. We're going to come back to this, but for now, just open the image in regular old Photoshop.

In order to get it ready to go, a few things need to be standardized. The first of these is that you want to be working with the proper DPI and dimensions to begin with so that you don't forget to do it later and run into unnecessary snags. Typical good image DPI is between 240 and 300, so go with 300. You can always size an image down more, but sizing back up can cause pixilation because you're literally removing information and then trying to add it back. The same is true of your dimensions. You always want to save a base file that's about as big as you'd ever want to print, so that your print image is nice and sharp. However, if for this project, that print size is smaller than your maximum desired image size, you can do one of two things. The first is, size it down to your desired image size, print, and then don't save that file, or save several versions of the image with different dimensions. This works well especially if you only have a range of two or three sizes that it gets printed at.

When you save your image changes, you want to keep it either as a DNG, or a TIFF file, because, again, these formats will allow you to have the most freedom with editing. You'll also want a JPEG copy for web use, and a Photoshop document copy to allow you to go back and make edits onto layers in the future.

If you also want borders on your image, now would be the time to do so, which you do in your Canvas Size menu, as opposed to the Image Size menu.

Finally, you need to decide on a color profile. Go to Edit>Color Settings and make sure the image profile working space for RGB is set to Adobe RGB (1998). Go to Edit>Assign Profile and make sure of the same, and then to Edit>Convert to profile, and make sure that the Source Space and Destination Space are both also set to Adobe RGB (1998). You may not think that this all affects very much right now, but on web and in print it certainly will. You'll also want to consider calibrating your monitor, which isn't a Photoshop thing, but can be found easily within the system preferences of your Mac, and, I would assume, your PC.

Now that your image is all standardized and ready to go, let's move into a comprehensive explanation of the tools to be found in Photoshop.

Chapter 2
Navigating the Toolbar

As a warning, this chapter may get a little bit exhaustive to read, but I promise it'll be worth it. It's all about your toolbar, and the functions of everything in it. I will indicate which tools you'll probably be using quite a lot with an asterisk, but will also give a brief overview of everything.

The first thing to know is that the toolbar is somewhat customizable, and that behind each base tool is a variant tool, which can be accessed when you press down on the button. It may take you a while to remember where everything is, but once you at least have an understanding of the base tools, you should be all right. All of the tools also have shortcuts that you will learn in time, and have their own settings toolbar which will run across the top of Photoshop beneath the main menu bar to allow you more options and easier accessibility as you switch between tools. Each tool also has its own shortcut, which you will memorize with use and time. Each is, of course, denoted by its own symbol, but these change as you click on variant tools. If you find yourself using a variant tool more than the main tool, you can leave it set like that. That, along with the specified toolbars, is where the customization comes in.

So here's the basic list, in bullet points, and I'll elaborate on the more commonly used tools as we go.

- **Move Tool:** This tool is self-explanatory. It allows you to move whatever you've got selected.

- **Rectangular Marquee Tool:** Allows you to make a rectangular selection when highlighted. If you hold down this button, you'll also find the options of elliptical, single row, and single column marquee tools.

- **Lasso Tool:** Opens up to the polygonal and magnetic lasso tools. These make more freely or weirdly shaped selections, and the magnetic lasso, true to its name, which will snap two edges it detects in the photo that it thinks you are trying to trace. Once you have made your selection, there is a box called Refine Edge that will become highlighted in your top toolbar. This will allow you to refine and tweak any part of the selection that may not be quite right, having selected too much or too little of an area.

- **Quick Selection Tool and Magic Wand:** This allows you to make a very quick selection for utilizing things like a quick mask, to map out where you're going. The edges won't be perfect, but like lasso, you can refine them. The variant tool, the Magic Wand, makes its quick selections based on tone and color in the image. Meaning that if you initially select something pink in an image, it will go and pick up on all the pinks. If you don't want it to pick up absolutely every shade of pink, but only a small section, play around with your tolerance at the top. You can also add to and take away from selections, as well as choose what type of sampling you would like to do and how many layers to sample, be it one or all of them.

- **Crop Tool:** The crop tool of course is self explanatory, but also gives way to the perspective crop tool, slice tool, and slice selection tool. The type of crops you make will depend on the realism and precision of your work, as well as whether you do any graphic design.

- **Eyedropper Tool:** The eyedropper tool allows you to select a foreground and background color, whether from the color picker, swatches, or your image. This tool can be especially helpful because it can allow you to greater match things like skin tones or gradients as you work and do corrections to small, specific areas. The Eyedropper tool gives way to a whole host of other tools: The 3D Material Eyedropper tool, the Color Sampler, the Ruler tool, the Note tool, and the Count tool. Of these, the only other one I really use is the Color Sampler, which allows you to select samples of up to four different colors within your image. This tool is extremely useful when trying to do color corrections, because you can set parameters to within those samples and make changes that way.

- **Spot Healing Brush Tool:** This tool and it's variants get a bunch of asterisks, because they are going to be very important and useful to you no matter what type of work you do. These are the tools that allow you to fix any sort of discrepancy or blemish imaginable, and for that, they're all going to get their own bullet points. So, Spot Healing Brush is awesome for things like blemishes in portraiture and dust on film. Because it is a brush, it has the same toolbar settings as the general brush tool, including brush size and firmness, blend modes, match modes, a sample all layers checkbox, and the swirly pen symbol, which allows you to match the brush pressure to its size.

- **Healing Brush Tool:** Does the same thing as the Spot Healing Brush, but over larger areas. However, with the Healing Brush Tool as with the Clone Tool, you have to select a sample spot to begin with and work from.

- **Patch Tool:** This will let you select an area within the photo that you would like to repair, using other pixels from another part of the photo to repair it. You simply select and drag the area over to correct it. This tool can also be used to clone isolated image areas.

- **Content Aware Move Tool:** Self-explanatory, it moves the selected area to wherever you drag it, but then uses the matching software to meld it almost effortlessly into its surroundings.

- **Red Eye Tool:** Removes red eye as caused by flash or other poor lighting conditions.

- The Brush Tool and its variants are also very, very essential. Obviously, the brush tool can be used for any kind of digital painting. Its control panel has an indicator and drop down menu for size, hardness, and shape of the brush, so you can really control it as you would an actual paintbrush. Next to that is a palette folder of all the brush presets that Photoshop includes. If you go into this dialog box, you can really have control over the type of brush you create. As you can see, you can control every aspect of the brush. This is really a tool that I would suggest taking the time to experiment with, both on photos and on blank Photoshop documents. If you happen to create a brush you really enjoy, you can add it to your list of presets here for quick access.

- **Pencil tool:** The Pencil Tool works essentially just like the brush tool, except that in my opinion, it's less versatile and more frustrating. Choose the Brush Tool over this all the time.

- **Color Replacement Tool:** It does exactly what it says: Gives you an easy way to change, or replace, the color of any element within a photo. What this tool does is takes a sample of the colors that are under the cursor, so make sure you set the size accordingly. Whatever color you're dragging over is the color you want to alter, and it will change to whatever your foreground color is set to. If you do move it outside of the area you intend to affect, it will affect that area too, unless you set the tolerance to make sure this doesn't happen. Just play around with that number until the tool is affecting only the areas you want it to. As mentioned before with the eyedropper tool, you can also choose to sample a complimenting color from the image instead of using the color picker.

- **Mixer Brush Tool:** I love, love, love the Mixer Brush Tool. It literally allows you to mix and blend your colors just as if it were a real paintbrush, and can add some awesome painterly effects to your images. You can decide how wet or dry you want the "paint" to look, and what you want the mix of colors to be, as in, how heavy on blue, or how light on the red, et cetera. There is also a drop down menu of presets for your convenience. Be careful though. This tool will cover your photograph unless you adjust it with the right opacity and blend modes to get the exact look you want.

- **Clone Stamp and Pattern Stamp Tool:** The Clone Stamp Tool is another great way to do retouching or to create any artistic patterns you might want. Clone Stamp allows you to select the area you would like to clone, and then click to apply it to other spots. The thing is that it works much better when being applied in close proximity with the spot of origin, and also works much better when being applied to small, selective spots. So set your brush size to the smallest size that you can possibly use for optimal results. The Pattern Stamp tool allows you to select preset patterns and apply them over your photos. As with other tools, you can also load other patterns of your choice for your use. You can either create your own and save them, or there are plenty of free and paid patterns online that are downloadable.

- **History Brush Tool:** The History Brush Tool works much the same as the history dialog box, except that, as its name implies, you can actually use it like a paintbrush to paint on the layer (and in the area) that you would like to undo. The Art History Brush tool does much the same thing as the History Brush tool, except that you can paint in filters or other under-layer effects, unlike the History Brush tool, which just allows you to undo things.

- **Eraser, Background Eraser, and Magic Eraser Tool:** The eraser and background eraser work exactly as their names imply, but the note I'd like to give you about these tools has to do with the concept of non-destructive editing. When you choose to use any of the eraser tools, you never want to erase right on your original image. Always use a copy or a layer, especially when using the background eraser tool. That way, if you want it back, you just have to click a button, and the same goes for if you make a mistake. The Magic Eraser tool is called that simply due to the fact that it is smart; it will select and erase pixels that are similar to the ones you designate.

- **Gradient, Paint Bucket, and 3D Material Drop Tool:** These tools kind of remind me a lot of paint on old, old Mac computers. They work almost exactly the same way. If you choose to apply a gradient, it may at first seem to obscure your entire image. But never fear, because you can isolate it on its own layer. That way, you can apply blend modes and differing opacities to allow lower layers to show through. Paint Bucket works exactly the way you might think, and is also similarly affected by blend modes and opacity. It will not fill your entire image when you click, however, but will follow the layout of your image depending on where you click. The 3D Material Drop tool is not something I've ever used before, because I don't work in 3D rendering, but basically what it does is allows you to drop uploaded textures into the picture, or rather, onto the 3D object.

- **Blur, Sharpen, and Smudge Tool:** These are pretty self-explanatory, and can be pretty useful for small fixes. The Smudge tool is really the most interesting in the way it makes things look, since, if heavily applied, it can have a melty, Surrealist effect.

- **Dodge, Burn, and Sponge Tool:** The dodge and burn tools work exactly like the traditional darkroom techniques of dodging, or allowing less light to effect parts of an image, and burning, or the opposite. Of course, it's a lot easier to do in Photoshop than it is in the darkroom, and there are even different settings that control how much you want the tool to affect the part of the image you're working on. The Sponge tool seems at first like it should be housed under another main spot, since the name reminds me a lot of the Pattern Stamp tool. But the name can be deceiving, and the Sponge tool is actually used to saturate or desaturate parts of your image.

- **Pen Tool:** This is mostly used for things like creating vector paths, although you can also draw with it. A path is sort of like an outline, it helps to map things out. The pen tool also houses the Freeform Pen Tool, and Add, Delete and Convert Anchor Point tools. This is because paths are made up of anchor points that tell it where to go.

- **Type Tool:** The type tool is awesome for any kind of graphic design process. With it, you can use Photoshop to create things like postcards or your own business cards.

- **Path Selection Tool:** Self-explanatory, this tool is great for use with the pen tool.

- **Shape Tools:** The shape tools are: the line tool, the ellipse tool, the rectangle tool, the polygon tool, and finally, the custom shape tool. Within the polygon tool and the custom shape tool are even more choices. Unlike the marquee tool, this tool doesn't create a selection space; it simply places the shape onto your image as its own layer.

- **Hand and Rotate View Tool:** The hand tool is useful for moving around within pictures when you're very zoomed into the frame. This will be especially helpful for things like retouching or restoration jobs. Rotate view allows you to rotate an image as little or as much as you like, and differs from the image rotation option in the image drop down menu because you can rotate by increments as opposed to by just 90 or 180 degrees.

- **Magnifying Glass:** It's just a glorified zoom tool. You can zoom by hitting Z and then clicking, but there's always good old command plus.

There's your brief run down of all the tools in Photoshop. Though that doesn't nearly cover every command that can be done via Photoshop, because we still need to cover things like the Filter Gallery and Layers, that's a good start on how to navigate and make things work for you. Speaking of making things work for you, one thing you will have to learn for yourself is which tools work best for what task. Generally speaking, there is no one way to perform a certain task, so you just have to figure out what your preferences are. You also have to figure out the best way to ensure that you're choosing the correct tool for a job. This can take some practice. However, research, experimentation, and knowing what questions to ask will help you as you continue to learn your way around Photoshop.

Chapter 3
Layers, Channels, and Paths

Layers

Let's talk about layers. One of the most fundamental rules when it comes to learning about Photoshop that I cannot stress enough is the importance of non-destructive editing. Non-destructive editing simply means that you use Photoshop properly—that is, to your advantage, to ensure you preserve all of the photographic and editing information that you can. That's where layers come in. Layers allow you to place each task that you perform in its own space.

In order to keep it all straight, especially when you've got over ten or so layers, Photoshop provides ways to keep it all organized. Firstly, you have your layer titles. There's no standardized way to title your layers, but you do want to make sure that you name each one. Use something that's going to trigger your memory, or the name of whatever fix you're trying to do. This way, if you should have to go back and change anything, you know exactly which layer you need to go to without having to click through every single one.

Photoshop also provides a way to see what your final image will look like with and without certain layers. You can tell if a layer is turned on or not by the checkbox next to the title. If a layer is on, or visible, there will be an eye symbol in the checkbox. If not, the checkbox will be empty. With this option, you can decide whether you want to keep or print a layer before you delete it for good.

If you want to organize your layers even more, you can also create layer groups, which will create a folder into which you can

17

drop all the layers you want. This is awesome for grouping like fixes. Say for example that you're retouching a portrait. You could have one grouping for eyes and lips, one for skin, one for hair, one for retouching wrinkles from fabric. You maybe thinking, how could I possibly need this many layers for something like that? But sometimes you want to do things in sections. For example, in the skin grouping, there maybe a separate layer for cheeks and for the forehead. The more layers you have, the less likely you are to get confused in the event of a mistake (that is, as to how to locate the mistake).

It may also be a good idea to group by what are necessary fixes, such as blemish removal or color correction, and to group by artistic choice. Later in the book, I will discuss modes that can be applied to layers to affect artistic choice even more. In the meantime, also in the same palette area as layers, are channels and paths.

Channels

Channels work in conjunction with mode, which can be found under the image tab. Mode reflects the type of color that your image is made up of, be it greyscale, RGB, or CMYK. RGB is an acronym for red, green, blue, while CMYK stands for cyan, magenta, yellow, and black, or the four colors used in print and layered to create full color. You can use channels for many things, including color corrections on each separate layer, or separated negatives, if you do any analog work. You can also use them to create more refined split toned images.

Paths

Your paths palette will appear as empty unless you have any paths in use. Remember, paths are created using the pen tool. When you do draw on a path, options will appear in the bottom toolbar. These are to fill the path, brush the path with your paintbrush, load the path as a selection, and conversely to make a path from a selection.

It's good that you are aware of what these tabs all do, because it will help you to utilize Photoshop the most, especially for more technical applications as you learn how to do more.

Chapter 4
Adjustment Layers

Adjustment layers work in conjunction with the general layers palette. Adjustment layers are just the fancy way of saying, all the correction you can do to a layer in order to get the most out of it. Basically, adjustment layers can be found in all of the menus, and you can select your corrections that way, but it's a lot more difficult to continually select from menu after menu. Discovering adjustment layers was one of the best things that ever happened in my journey with Photoshop.

You can easily locate your adjustment layers one of two ways. In both the Essentials and the Photography workspaces, you will remember that there is a tab in the top of your palette layered Adjustments. When you click this, you will see several rows of symbols. Alternatively, you can use the toolbar down at the bottom of the palette, where adjustment layers are housed under a drop down menu represented by what looks like a half shaded circle.

Within the adjustment palette, each symbol represents an adjustment layer, or type of layer. They are the following: Levels, Brightness/Contrast, Exposure, Curves, Vibrance, Color balance, Hue/Saturation, Photo Filter, Black and White, Channel Mixer, Invert, Color Lookup, Threshold, Posterize, Gradient map and Selective Color. When you use one of these layers, it is pre-labeled as to its function. The other plus to the adjustment layers as opposed to going through the main menus is that each correction automatically has its own layer, whereas through the main menu the correction gets *applied.* I find adjustment layers to be less destructive and feel that they make it easier to track and fine tune changes.

In my opinion, some of these are more essential than others, and even though they are pretty self-explanatory, I would still like to go through each one and provide a visual example. I'm just going to work my way down the list.

So, when you click on an adjustment layer, the layer forms within the layers palette, and a properties box also pops up. This is where you control your adjustment.

Brightness and Contrast

The wonderful thing about adjustment layers, too, is that it automatically includes a layer mask so that you can control, within the layer, where the adjustment will be applied. Brightness and Contrast are controls that should be used sparingly, because they are not as refined as some of the other choices that you have. You don't want to push either one of these too high, because it will just make your photo look unprofessional. In fact, if you are going to use the brightness and contrast sliders, I would suggest applying then after you apply any changes using the exposure slider for the Levels and Curves slider. This way, you are not tempted to make your photos look so high contrast that it becomes crunchy. Even so with these warnings, let's take a look at what the Brightness and Contrast sliders look like when applied to an image. Pull up one of your own images that needs little to no correction applied. Use the original for comparison and just play around with the sliders, saving different versions of them. You may not think that the tools are making that much of a difference, but when you pull up your altered images alongside the original, you will see how even a small five point change makes a huge difference. Don't believe me? Try it on a few different images and see what you get. Try making a version where you just minimally pop up contrast and brightness. This is good editing, generally. Then make a version of the image in which you push the changes to their max, which is an example of what not to do in most cases.

In your second image, the sliders should have barely moved. What you are generally looking for in your corrections is subtlety.

Then take a look at your third image, which is what the same image would look like if you were to push the contrast slider all the way up to 100. This is a common mistake that many new photographers make, especially when they get excited with Photoshop. They want their images to stand out, and look punchy, but instead, the effect is not exciting, it's just unprofessional. You can tell with most images that pushing the contrast all the way is not the way to go, because your white highlights will get blown out. The histogram at the top of Photoshop will also appear very striated, as opposed to the smooth overlap of the colors in the histogram of the original (assuming the original was a well exposed and balanced photograph to start with).

Levels

Levels are definitely my favorite way to control the light in an image. Firstly, the levels dialog provides you with a histogram so that you can see the light and dark levels of your original photo, and visually track the changes as you make them. Take a close look at what your levels histogram looks like with your original photo. If you chose well, the initial histogram should already be pretty well-balanced. This means that any changes you choose to do will be more in an artistic vein as opposed to a corrective one.

As you can see, levels has two sliders, the top of which is for shadows, midtones and highlights. This is where we want to focus first. If you already know the area in which the correction needs to be done, for example, if you just want a little bit more punch in the midtones as we do here, start with that tic on the slider. In this case, of course, that is the middle one. Remember, less is more.

Here's another scenario. Let's say that you want to be able to make the green in a photo even darker, but you're afraid of how else it will affect the other colors in your photo that you don't want it to. You could just bump up the saturation, but keep in mind that this will provide a slightly different green rather than darkening. So, in order to darken, just apply a layer mask. What layer masks do is either allow or block a change from a certain area that you specify. This is where your foreground and background colors and the highlighting of the layer mask come in. You need to make sure that:

- Your foreground and background colors are set to black and white. It doesn't really matter which is which, because you can reverse them by hitting the X key. Black will block an adjustment from affecting an area, and white will allow it.

- Your layer mask, (or the white rectangle featured within the layer), is selected as opposed to the layer itself. If it isn't, when you paint, you'll just be applying unwanted color directly onto your image.

Assuming these things are done, you're ready to go. So let's apply the mask to the flowers. Considering how small the tulips are within the frame, you'll most likely want to zoom in until they are large enough to be adequately painted on without accidentally painting into other areas of the frame. Set your foreground color to black, and paint away. As you paint, the change will not show up on the image itself, but rather, you will see black shapes of where you've painted begin to appear on the white of the layer mask. Keep in mind that you'll want to work with more care and precision, for a finished photo, although for this exercise, you can just go quickly. If you're working on a laptop, investing in a mouse or even a tablet to draw on can help with more detail-oriented work.

Now, apply your change. If you aren't too precise in masking, you can see little rings around areas you masked as you push your midtones. However, this is an easy fix. Just hit X, which will switch your foreground to white, and brush back over it.

Curves

Curves perform essentially the same function as levels, but are even more precise. Within this dialog box the corrections are interactive, meaning that you can click anywhere within the histogram that you need to, moving the guiding line up or down to adjust highlights and shadows. You can also make more than one point on the line to affect more than one change at a time in an image.

Like levels, you can also use the mask to make sure that the layer only affects parts in the image that you want it to. Another easy way to make sure that you're getting exactly what you need is to use the eyedropper tools to sample the area where you want the blacks, midtones and whites to come from. This can take some practice however, because if you select something that is too dark for example, you can get some weird color casts on your image. This is just one of those tools as you are old as you're playing around with this practice to get it just right. As you're playing around with this, however it will get easier to use, and you may just discover some practical and artistic applications for it. This way, your final image has more color and contrast than it did, but it isn't overdone or oversaturated. Feel free to experiment with your own photos, and start with some that you know need some obvious fixes, then move into more subtle fixes that require a much lighter hand. Breaking away from just talking about each type of adjustment layer separately, I want to talk about what you can do with adjustment layers now that you've got a good base file to work from.

Photo Filters

The photo filters adjustment layer is a throwback from the world of analog photography. When you went to take an analog photo before the days of Photoshop, fixes couldn't be done to the negatives after the fact. So, if for example, you needed to shoot a landscape and pop your greens to be more vibrant, you could use a green filter. Same with if you needed to bring in clouds, although that would require a different kind of filter, blue, I believe. These photo filter adjustments can help you to bring in or pop anything you need after the fact, and even if your photo isn't really in need of a fix, you can also use them to affect the color of the lighting, making it warmer or cooler, or more neutral, et cetera. This will affect the overall mood of the photograph to be read the way you want it to. For example, in relationship to landscape photography you can add a green filter to make sure the color is as rich as it should be. However, as you can see if you apply it, it will affect the whole picture, so again, make use of your layer masks as well, unless you find yourself preferring the overall look.

Selective Color

Let's move on to more color correction adjustment layers that could potentially be used for creative applications. Now, this probably isn't the selective color you've been thinking of. It's not where you can take an image and turn it all black and white and save for one part. We're going to cover that skill, as well as how to color in black and white images, in the next installment. Instead, this adjustment layer is a way of affecting the colors in your color balance via adjusting the mix of CMYK. First, you have to choose whether you want the dialog box to operate under a preset or custom. Personally, with any slider that offers a preset, I like to use that only as a starting point, and then adjust, which then of course, makes it custom, but allows you to make some finer adjustments than just a preset would. Next, you'll need to decide what color you'd like to affect. Odds are, unless you've got one definite color cast, you'll have to adjust a second color after you correct the first. One of the things I'd like to fix in this photo is very minor, but this goes back to learning how to edit for subtlety. It's that the reddish tulips, while very red in real life, did not translate very well within the photograph. So, let's set the colors to reds. The reason you can still use all the sliders (cyan, magenta, yellow and black) is because all of these colors are still going to affect the reds and be affected by the reds.

Also pay attention to whether you've got the relative or absolute bubble checked at the bottom of the dialog box. This is going to affect your colors. Relative means, anything that is relatively within that range of green is going to be affected, while absolute is every green within that range getting affected. Check both and switch back and forth to see which one you like better. As you can see with this image, the grass becomes more yellow when you check absolute as opposed to relative. So this tool is one way to do your color corrections, although for tougher fixes, I would suggest the good old color balance tool.

Color Balance

This is a great tool for when you have a good image that has just a bit too much of a certain color (or two). The color balance dialog automatically starts out with the midtones sliders checked, but that doesn't mean that that's what you have to start with. Take a look at the photo and see if you can determine where you need a fix. Is your image too yellow, green, blue, or magenta? Is it too much so in highlights, midtones, or shadows? Where needs the most help, and where needs just a nudge? Keep in mind as you change one component that you will be affecting the relationships of the others, and less is more, to start out with, generally.

I understand that all of these changes are very subtle and you're probably looking at the pictures, going, "I don't see the difference . . . ," but I promise it's there. The important thing with anything in Photoshop is that you *don't* have to do everything in post. If you think this way, you're going to be stuck working in Photoshop for a very long time, getting frustrated, and probably giving up. Granted, some of the processes that will be addressed later are very work intensive and can take hours, but something like color correction shouldn't. If things like your color corrections are subtle, that likely means that you're doing a great job of making sure everything is working well in camera. But because color changes can, and should, be so subtle, you really will want to make sure that your monitor is calibrated correctly. That way, if you have to use another computer to print or edit, you won't get on and be completely shocked if your color balance is entirely off. Of course, you should always check that any monitor you work on is correctly calibrated.

While there are other adjustment layers to be spoken about, I feel that the most important ones that will get the most use have been thoroughly covered. This chapter is very important to understanding the basics because all of these adjustment layers are going to be vital in the processes you'll learn later.

Chapter 5
Blend Modes

Blend modes are really fun, because they allow you to meld together as many layers as you want into one cohesive piece. There's really no one way to go about talking about blend modes, because there are so many of them and because they all affect each other differently depending upon a multitude of factors, including but not limited to, each photo you're working with, how many layers you're working with, other blend modes that have been applied, and what opacities you have each blend mode and layer set to.

Let's get started with a list of what each of the blend modes are, and in order to demonstrate what each one does with nothing else applied to it, I'm just going to make a copy of my current picture and apply the blend modes to the top layer. Some blend modes will work better with different images underneath, as opposed to the same.

First of all, to access your blend modes, go up to the top of your layers palette, to the drop down menu, which, at present, should read "normal." When you click on the menu, you will see that the blend modes are separated by the task that they perform. These include darkening, lightening, light quality, options that will make it look like a negative, and color considerations.

First is dissolve, which will give your image a crackled look. It doesn't really show up on two layers of the same image, so here it is just applied to one layer. And below that, are two images blended together using this mode. I've never really used dissolve for any corrective purposes, but it does have a nice painterly, glazed effect. If you choose to include a second, different image, just be aware that fill and opacity will affect how the image looks, and that there is no possible way for me to show you all of the effects it could have. But blend modes are really a lot of fun to play around with, so get in Photoshop and have some fun. You never know what you might come up with. Also, if you're wondering how to create a second layer with a different picture, all you have to do is open your second picture, and then go to its tab. Grab the picture or section of the picture that you want with the marquee tool and press command C to copy. Then, when you get back to your initial image, hit command V to paste. If you need to rearrange your layers, simply drag them around within the layers palette until you're satisfied.

Next are the darkening blend modes, and as you will see, some will look very similar to others. They are: Darken, Multiply, Color Burn, Linear Burn, and Darker Color.

You might be wondering why the one labeled darker color is actually lighter than some of the other darkened images. My guess would be that the other images are darker because they involve a burn or in analog photography the process of adding more time to a certain part of the picture. Whereas with darker color there is no burn involved, just a general darkening of the image.

Just as with the above darken blend modes, the lightening blend modes, only lighten color if it is a color dodge, whereas lighter color and screen affect the entire image overall not just the parts most affected by saturated color.

With this section of blend modes, the types of light are affected as you can see something like soft light is going to give you a very soft picture with emphasis on the second layer. Alternatively, at least with this set of images the harsher lights such as hard mix and pin light put more emphasis on the top image. These harsher blend modes can be good if you are going for a posterized, graphic design kind of feel. However, if you are sticking with straight up photographic techniques, you might want to go easy on these blend modes and lower their opacity.

Difference, Exclusion, Subtract, Divide

With this section of blend modes, I will be honest and say that I'm not entirely sure how they work, and also that I have never found much use for application of them. With these particular images, I still don't find that they work very well, however I know that on some images they can create a look that is quite like a negative, be it color or black and white. My guess is that the algorithm works by excluding certain parts of the layer. For example, with difference it looks like the intensity of the top image was kept but not the information from the image itself. Exclusion looks like the top image was left out entirely and also that all contrast and saturation got taken away from the bottom image. So again this is just one of those times when I would tell you that it depends upon what you need and it's really easy to scroll through blend modes to see if any of them will work for what you are doing.

Hue, Saturation, Color, Luminosity

These blend modes principally affect the color and all the attributes of color within the two images being used. As you can see, if the colors of the photographs are not similar enough it can result in some weird color casts when using the color blending mode. But if the luminosity or shine of the image is similar the two will blend together to make one new entity quite effortlessly. Saturation is a good tool to use if you are ever having trouble popping up your colors using the saturation slider. This way, the blend mode will get you pretty close to where you need to be, and you can perform the last little tweaks manually to get it perfect.

Also in the layers palette are a bunch of symbols down at the bottom which relate to layer masks and adding more layers. But there is also a drop down menu labeled FX, which gives you even more options for blending. While these are not strictly blend modes in the same way the others are, they provide you with the ability to add even more depth by adding texture or shadows to your image. In the beginning of the next part of this book I will start out with the uses and applications of the FX drop down menu, before moving into how you begin to accomplish specific tasks within Photoshop.

Conclusion

Remember, this is just the start of your journey into understanding how Photoshop works. Make sure you're having fun as you go, and don't stress out. I think one of the biggest lessons I've learned about using Photoshop is not to wait until you have a deadline or the necessity of a certain skill to learn it. I've also learned that, while assignments, be they for school or a client or just personal, are good learning experiences, they aren't enough for that to be the only time you practice. You have to get yourself into the habit of taking pictures just to practice on.

While Photoshop is commonly thought of as a tool for fixing mistakes, I want readers of this book to shift that thinking right now and see it as a tool for enhancement. What I mean by this is that you shouldn't rely on the possibility that, "I can fix it in post" to allow you to skate by with subpar pictures in camera that then become okay pictures in Photoshop. Rather, think this: That your pictures should be printable and useable straight from your camera with only minor tweaks, and then when you put them in Photoshop, they become magical because you know exactly what tools to use to pull the most from each image you choose to use. Begin to shift your thinking to considering Photoshop as a tool for applying artistic, aesthetic choices and completely transforming your images from good photos to multimedia digital works of art. There is almost literally no limit to the creative processes and layers you can use within Photoshop to create almost anything you'd want.

Something you will learn, however, is that it is essential to work from extremely high quality materials from the start. You can always make a photo smaller or change the file type to a less hefty one for web use, but you can't take a tiny file and make it bigger without losing a lot of resolution and a lot of professional credibility. Also, while it is entirely possible to do some pretty crazy things within Photoshop, such as removal of people or objects, body reshaping, and face swapping, there are limits, because Photoshop works within an algorithm of possibility, not magical thinking. One of the craziest things I have ever been asked, for example, was whether I could make a person who was stationary in a photograph look like they were jumping. The answer to that, if you apply common sense, is a resounding no. As you learn what is possible and what isn't, you will gain more of an appreciation for retouching and the general art of post processing.

In this book, you have learned how to prep your images, how to find your way around the toolbar, which tools are useful for what, and how to use and combine adjustment layers and blend modes to get the most out of your image, or out of multiple images. Keep in mind that everything I've gone through here today are just suggestions and starting points, and that the possibilities, even just with adjustment layers and blend modes, really are endless. If you don't understand them at first, don't use that as a reason to get discouraged and not make use of them. Just continue to push your limits and explore.

In the next installment of these Photoshop books, we will be delving into more complex processes, and they are going to involve much more work for you than just the occasional screenshot to show you what I mean. The focus will be on a combination of portrait and fashion retouching, and how to utilize different modes and extensions, such as HDR, the Liquefy tool, and the filter gallery for artistic, impressionistic applications.

Did you Like "Photoshop"?

Before you go, I'd like to say thank you so much for purchasing my book.

I know you could have picked from dozens of books on this subject, but you took a chance with mine, and I'm truly grateful for that.

So, once again, a big thanks for downloading this book and reading all the way to the end—I truly appreciate it.

Now I'd like to ask for a small favor if you don't mind:

Would you be so kind as to take a minute of your time and leave a review for this book on Amazon?

This feedback will help me continue to write the kind of books that help you get results. And if you loved it, then please feel free to let me know! :)

More Books by James Carren

Portrait Photography - 9 Tips Your Camera Manual Never Told You About Portrait Photography

Landscape Photography - 10 Essential Tips to Take Your Landscape Photography to The Next Level

Photography Lighting - Top 10 Must-Know Photography Lighting Facts to Shoot Like a Pro in Your Home Studio

Photography For Beginners - From Beginner To Expert Photographer In Less Than a Day!

Photography Business: 20 Things You Need to Know Before Starting a Successful Photography Business

www.ingramcontent.com/pod-product-compliance
Lightning Source LLC
Chambersburg PA
CBHW071016180526
45168CB00003B/1441